BY VALERIE BODDEN

CREATIVE EDUCATION

Published by Creative Education
P.O. Box 227, Mankato, Minnesota 56002
Creative Education is an imprint of The Creative Company
www.thecreativecompany.us

Design and production by The Design Lab
Art direction by Rita Marshall
Printed by Corporate Graphics in the United States of America

Photographs by 123RF (Natalia Bratslavsky, Charles Shapiro),
Alamy (Inge Johnsson, Tom Till, Jim West), Corbis (Tom
Bean, Lester Lefkowitz), Dreamstime (Dallasphotography,
Dkarlsson, Jjmullen, Poco_bw, Tank_bmb, Tashka, Tsz01),
iStockphoto (Angelo Elefante, Eric Foltz, Mike Norton)

Library of Congress Cataloging-in-Publication Data
Bodden, Valerie.
Grand Canyon / by Valerie Bodden.
p. cm. — (Big outdoors)
Summary: A fundamental introduction to the Grand Canyon,
including the deserts and forests that surround it, the creatures that
live in it, and how people have affected its arid environment.
Includes index.
ISBN 978-1-58341-815-4
1. Grand Canyon (Ariz.)—Juvenile literature. I. Title. II. Series.

F788.B65 2010
979.1'32—dc22   2009004688

CPSIA: 051910 PO1278
9 8 7 6 5 4 3 2

BIG OUTDOORS
GRAND CANYON

NORTH
AMERICA

The Grand
Canyon is a
huge canyon.
A canyon is a long,
narrow strip of low land
surrounded by higher
land. The Grand Canyon
is in the state of Arizona.
The Colorado River flows
through it.

The Colorado River starts in Colorado and makes its way to the canyon

The Grand Canyon is so big that it can be seen from outer space.

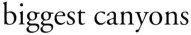

The Grand Canyon is one of the biggest canyons in the world. It is 277 miles (446 km) long. Most of the canyon is about one mile (1.6 km) deep. High stone cliffs surround the Grand Canyon.

The canyon looks different from close up and from high above

Scientists think that the Grand Canyon was created by the Colorado River. The river slowly cut through the rocky ground to form the canyon. Then wind, rain, and ice made it wider.

Even in the winter, the Colorado River (above) keeps flowing

The Colorado River is 100 feet (30 m) deep in some places.

The Grand Canyon is made up of many layers of different-colored rock.

The weather at the Grand Canyon's **rims** is warm in the summer and cold in the winter. Inside the canyon are hot, dry **deserts**. There are many towns near the canyon's rims. But some **American Indians** live in villages at the bottom of the canyon.

Much of the canyon land is dry and rocky, with few big plants

There are forests along the Grand Canyon's rims. Squirrels, mountain lions, and black bears live there. Bald eagles fly above the canyon.

Bald eagles eat fish from the river, and squirrels find nuts and seeds

About 200 different kinds of birds live in the Grand Canyon.

The Grand Canyon's cacti and other plants are food for desert tortoises.

Cacti grow near where desert bighorn sheep, snakes, and spiders live in the canyon. Cottonwood trees grow along parts of the Colorado River, too.

Mountain goats and tortoises eat many plants found in the canyon

American Indians
have lived in the
Grand Canyon
for a long time. The
first white people saw the
canyon almost 500 years
ago. At first, they did not
want to explore it. But later
the Grand Canyon became
popular with visitors.

Early Indians made their homes in the rock and drew pictures, too

Sometimes people hurt the Grand Canyon. Some visitors leave garbage on the ground. Power companies that make electricity **pollute** the air. But many people are working to protect the Grand Canyon today.

Most people climb on the canyon's rocks without hurting anything

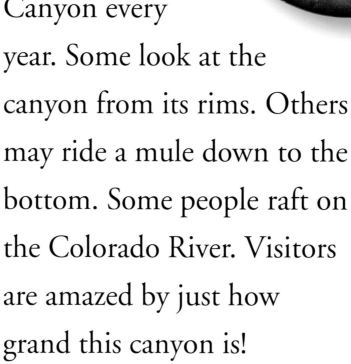

Lots of people visit the Grand Canyon every year. Some look at the canyon from its rims. Others may ride a mule down to the bottom. Some people raft on the Colorado River. Visitors are amazed by just how grand this canyon is!

Rafting on the river and riding mules are two ways to see the canyon

A **dam** above the Grand Canyon slows the flow of the Colorado River.

Glossary

American Indians people who lived in America before white people arrived

cacti desert plants that have spines (sharp spikes) instead of leaves; a single plant is called a cactus

dam a wall built across a river to hold water back

deserts big, hot areas sometimes covered with sand

pollute to make dirty with chemicals or other things that are bad for the earth, water, or air

rims the high lands that are at the edge of the Grand Canyon

Read More about It

Bauer, Marion Dane. *The Grand Canyon.* New York: Aladdin, 2006.

Trumbauer, Lisa. *Grand Canyon.* New York: Children's Press, 2005.

Index